Featherstone

CW00558202

50 fantastic ideas for mark making

ALISTAIR BRYCE-CLEGG

Featherstone Education
An imprint of Bloomsbury Publishing Plc

50 Bedford Square
London
WC1B 3DP
UK

1385 Broadway
New York
NY 10018
USA

www.bloomsbury.com

FEATHERSTONE and the Feather logo are trademarks of Bloomsbury Publishing Plc

First published 2015

A catalogue record for this book is available from the British Library.

ISBN
PB: 978-1-4729-1324-1
ePDF: 978-1-4729-1912-0

4 6 8 10 9 7 5 3

Typeset by Newgen Knowledge Works (P) Ltd., Chennai, India
Printed and bound in India by Replika Press Pvt. Ltd.

This book is produced using paper that is made from wood grown in managed, sustainable forests. It is natural, renewable and recyclable. The logging and manufacturing processes conform to the environmental regulations of the country of origin.

Contents

Introduction

All children have a desire to make marks... with fingers, sticks, crayons, felt tips... the list is endless! There is something very empowering about being able to leave your own mark.

Our aim should be to encourage our children to engage in and enjoy the process of making as many different marks as possible, in as many different ways as possible. The more textural experiences that we can add into the process, the more engaging the mark making will be and the more the children will want to do it.

Young babies will start the process of mark making in their high chairs when they are experimenting with the texture of their food and the discovery of the world around them. It is this curiosity and experience that eventually takes their early mark making into writing.

It is important to remember that mark making and writing is about so much more than learning letter shapes and sounds and then picking up a pencil. Those skills are difficult enough on their own, but when you try and do them all at once it is little wonder that some children would rather do anything than write!

The most important step of all is to recognise how our children are inspired and motivated to learn, and to then use this information to create exciting and purposeful opportunities for them to mark make and eventually write.

In this book I have gathered together a range of activities that will encourage children to make their marks in a variety of different ways. Even though the book has been split into 50 individual 'activities', the idea behind each activity can be used in several different contexts and a number of different ways. Just let your (and your children's) imagination loose to open up a whole new world of possibilities when it comes to exciting mark making!

Food allergy alert

FOOD allergy !

When using food stuffs to enhance the children's play opportunties, always be mindful of potential food allergies. Look out for this symbol on the relevant pages.

Skin allergy alert

SKIN allergy !

Some detergents and soaps can cause skin reactions. Always be mindful of potential skin allergies when letting the children mix anything with their hands, and always provide hand-washing facilities for the children to wash materials off after they have been in contact with skin. Watch out for this symbol on the relevant pages.

Safety issues

Social development can only take place when children are given opportunities to experiment and take reasonable risks in a safe environment. Encouraging independence and the use of natural resources inevitably raises some health and safety issues; these are identified where appropriate.

Children need help and good models for washing their hands when using natural materials or preparing food. They may need reminding not to put things in their mouths, and to be careful with real-life or found resources.

Sparkle dust

What you need:

- **Table salt**
- **Ziplock bag**
- **Food colouring**
- **Essential oils** (for scent)
- **Bowl, sand tray or mirror**
- **Glitter**
- **Dried flowers** (such as lavender or rose petals)

What to do:

1. Put the table salt into a ziplock bag.
2. Add three or four drops of your chosen food colouring.
3. Add three or four drops of your chosen essential oil and close the bag.
4. Move the salt around inside the bag, squeezing the mixture until the salt is fully coated and coloured.
5. Empty into a bowl or sand tray, or onto a mirror.
6. Sprinkle with glitter.
7. Add dried flowers and petals.

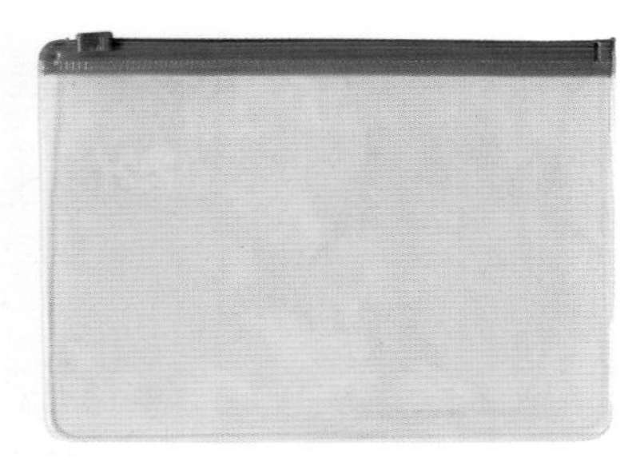

Taking it forward

Have a go at:

- Making lots of different bags of salt, themed around children's colour and scent preferences.
- Let the children make marks and patterns in the salt with their fingers, or with utensils such as paintbrushes.

What's in it for the children?

The children will enjoy the texture of the salt and find it easy to manipulate. If you theme the activity around the children's preferences you should get high level engagement.

Health & Safety

Never leave children unsupervised with essential oils.

Magic blackboard

What you need:

- **Blackboard**
- **Chalk** (different sizes)
- **Water**
- **Paintbrushes** (different sizes)

What to do:

1. The adult uses chalk to draw patterns, shapes or letters onto the blackboard.
2. The children move a paintbrush dipped in water over the chalk mark making.
3. The chalk mark making disappears!

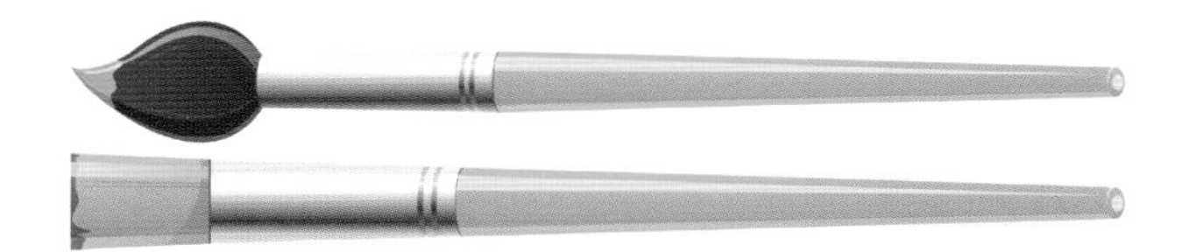

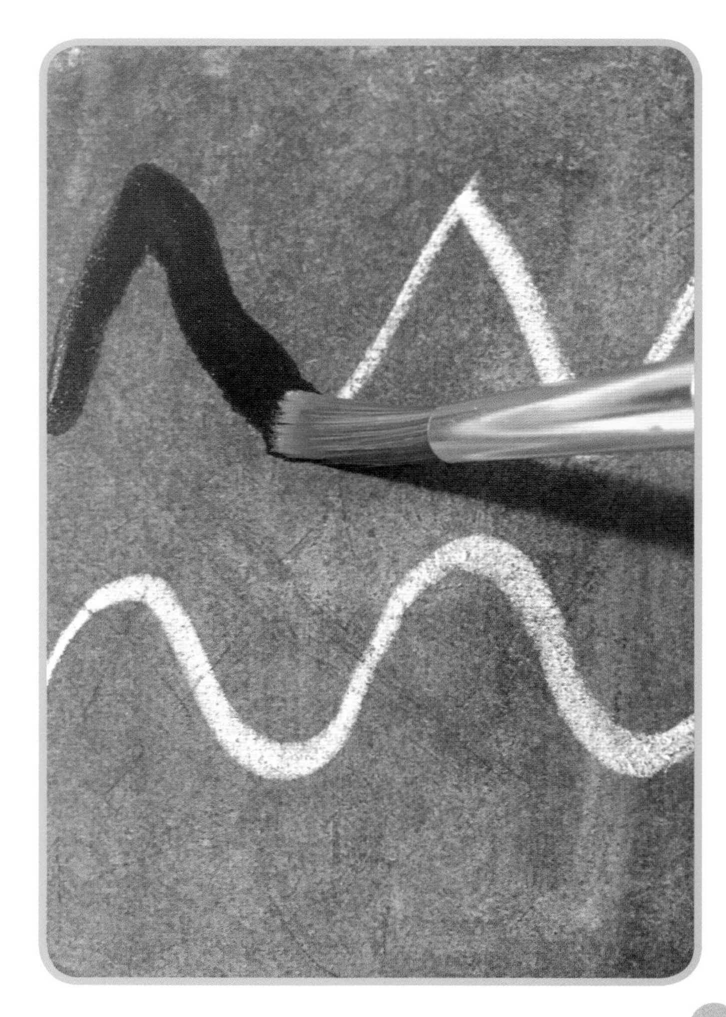

Taking it forward

Have a go at:

- Inviting the children to do the initial chalk mark making, using different-sized chalks.
- Encouraging the children to use different-sized paintbrushes for the water stage.
- Providing sponges of various sizes, in case any of the children find it difficult to manipulate the paintbrushes.

What's in it for the children?

The children will be developing their gross and fine motor skills as well as hand-eye coordination, spatial awareness and, in some cases, letter orientation.

Snow

What you need:

- **A snowy day** (if a snowy day isn't available, see 'Summer Snow' on page 26)
- **String and sticks** (optional)
- **Water-based paints**
- **Paintbrushes and sponges**

What to do:

1. If you think it's necessary, use the string and sticks to mark out a 'canvas' in the snow.
2. Let the children mark make with the watercolour paint, experimenting with different-sized paintbrushes and sponges.
3. Encourage them to 'draw' on the snow, as well as holding the brush still and allowing the colour to seep into the snow.

Taking it forward

Have a go at:

- Putting a watered-down paint solution into a spray bottle for a different effect.

What's in it for the children?

This can be a very sensory experience for children. They will experience the temperature of the snow, the colour of the paint and the changing state of the snow as it melts and the colours mix.

Laminated faces

What you need:

- Digital camera
- Printer
- Laminator
- Dry-wipe marker pens

What to do:

1. Take a 'head and shoulders' photograph of the children (and you).
2. Blow it up to A4 size.
3. Print the photograph.
4. Laminate it.
5. Let the children draw on their own faces or the faces of their friends, using dry-wipe markers!

Taking it forward

Have a go at:

- Using magazines, if you don't have photos of your own children.
- Encouraging the children to create disguises using glasses, patches, hats, moustaches and beards!

What's in it for the children?

There is a high level of engagement with this activity – the children always find it hilarious to be able to graffiti themselves or their friends!

Blackboard table

What you need:

- A small table
- Blackboard paint
- Paintbrushes and/or small paint rollers
- Chalk

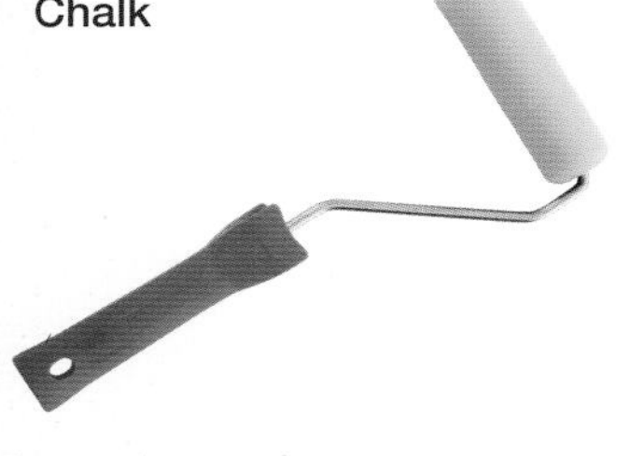

What to do:

1. Cover all of the table with blackboard paint, including the table legs and underside.
2. Use a roller to achieve a really smooth and even finish.
3. Once dry, allow the children to use the chalk to mark make all over the table surface.

Taking it forward

Have a go at:

- Using the blackboard paint to paint other objects for children to mark make on, such as stones, plant pots, boxes and crates.
- Allow the children to remove the chalk marks using water and paintbrushes once they have finished the activity, so that the table once again has a blank surface ready for next time!

What's in it for the children?

The children will enjoy the freedom of being able to mark make anywhere on the table. Mark making down the legs and on the underside of the table will encourage children to use lots of different muscle groups, as well as developing their hand-eye coordination.

Takeaway tray

What you need:

- Takeaway or polystyrene trays
- Scissors
- Objects that will make an indentation, such as a pizza wheel, dough modelling tools, or blunt pencils

What to do:

1. Cut each takeaway tray in half along the 'hinge'.
2. Encourage the children to create patterns and marks in the bottom of their tray using the tools you have provided.

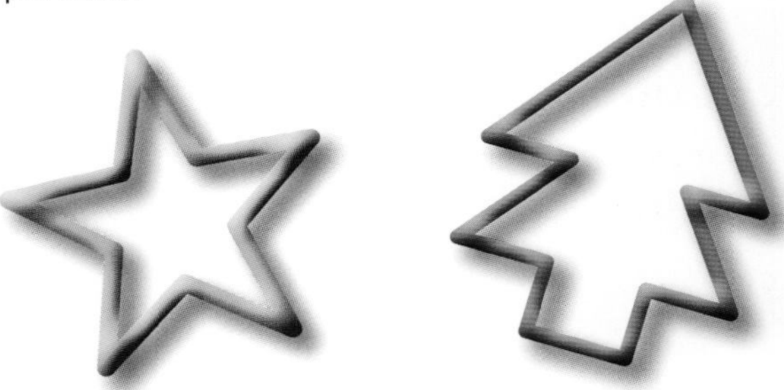

Taking it forward

Have a go at:

- Sourcing larger surfaces for the children to work on, such as thick cardboard or polystyrene tiles.
- Using the indentations to create a mono print (see activity on page 38).

What's in it for the children?

Not only are the children creating marks with their tools, they are required to apply pressure to create the indentations and this in turn will help to develop their strength of grip and their motor control.

Mark making mirror

What you need:

- **Mirror** (large or small)
- **A selection of any substances, e.g. paint, shaving foam, soap, whiteboard markers, sand, tea leaves and coffee granules** (the list is endless)
- **Mark making tools such as paintbrushes, sticks, sponges and fingers**
- **Digital camera**

What to do:

1. Place your mirror on a secure horizontal surface.
2. Empty your chosen substance onto the mirror.
3. Encourage the children to use their fingers or tools to create shapes and patterns.
4. Photograph the end result.

Taking it forward

- Try positioning several mirrors next to each other to create a collage.

What's in it for the children?

There is something very engaging for the children about being able to see themselves making marks. The fact that their mark making is reflected in the mirror will help them with control and formation, and makes a great talking point!

Top tip ★

If you don't want to use real glass then plastic mirror sheeting works just as well.

Smelly pictures

What you need:

- Sandpaper
- Scented tea lights

What to do:

1. Peg the sandpaper on an easel or lay on a flat surface.
2. Let the children draw or mark make on the sandpaper, using the tea lights as wax markers.
3. Once finished, encourage them to sniff their artwork!

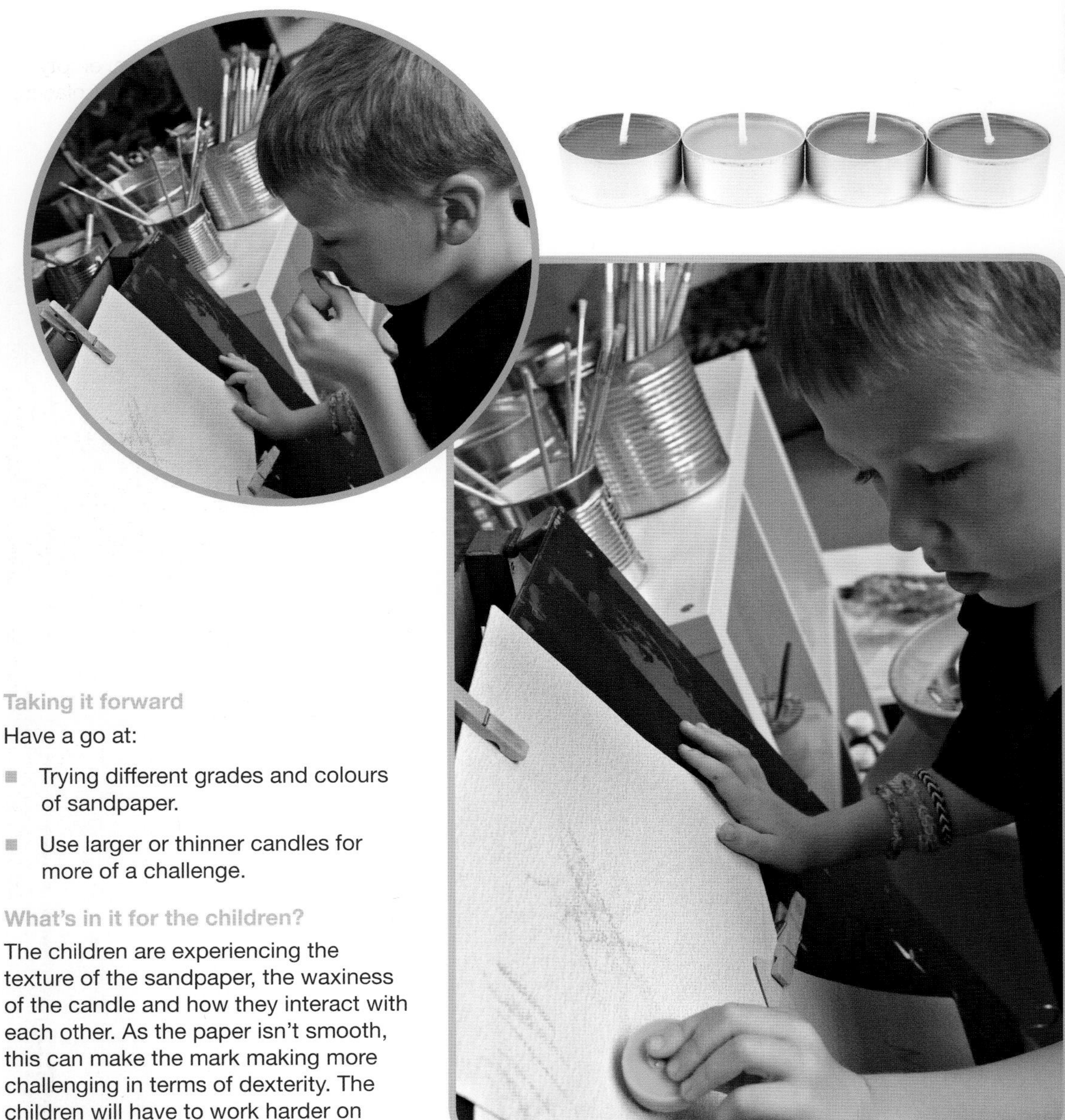

Taking it forward

Have a go at:

- Trying different grades and colours of sandpaper.
- Use larger or thinner candles for more of a challenge.

What's in it for the children?

The children are experiencing the texture of the sandpaper, the waxiness of the candle and how they interact with each other. As the paper isn't smooth, this can make the mark making more challenging in terms of dexterity. The children will have to work harder on their motor control.

Rainbow bubble writing

What you need:

- Washing up bowl
- Cup of water
- Washing-up liquid
- Food colouring
- Electric whisk
- Large activity tray or sheet of plastic

What to do:

1. Put one cup of water into your washing-up bowl.
2. Add a generous squirt of washing-up liquid.
3. Add a few drops of food colouring (depending on intensity of colour).
4. Whisk!
5. Once you have a bowl full of coloured bubbles, empty them out into your activity tray or onto a sheet of plastic.
6. Repeat the process, using a different colour.
7. Get mark making in your lovely bubbly mixture!

Taking it forward

- If you want more bubbles, just add more water and whisk again.
- Add glitter to make a sparkly bubble mix.

What's in it for the children?

The children will enjoy the experience of using the whisk. There is lots of potential for speech and language development through discussion about how the mountains of coloured bubbles are created.

Soil trays

What you need:

- Soil (**not** compost)
- Water
- Wooden or plastic trays (various sizes)
- Various natural items to make marks with, e.g. sticks, shells, feathers
- Inspirations for mark making, e.g. patterns and designs

Health & Safety

Always wash hands after handling natural materials.

What to do:

1. Mix the soil with a little water so that it becomes denser.
2. Fill the trays with the soil mixture.
3. Invite the children to use the natural objects to make marks in the soil. They may wish to look at a few repeating patterns in nature for inspiration.

Taking it forward

Have a go at:

- Adding sand to the soil for some extra texture.
- Providing other natural materials for children to decorate and enhance their patterns.

What's in it for the children?

Soil can be quite soft or dense, depending on how much water you add. This activity will give the children a different level of resistance to their mark making tools, requiring them to use different amounts of pressure to create their marks.

Overhead projector doodles

What you need:

- Overhead projector (OHP)
- Sheets of acetate
- Acetate pens (or permanent markers)
- A flat surface or wall

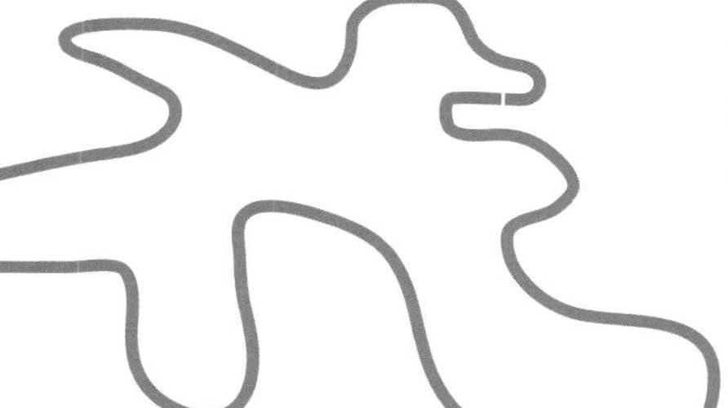

What to do:

1. Set up your OHP.
2. Put a sheet of acetate onto the flat bed of the OHP.
3. Let the children mark make onto the acetate, using the markers.
4. The children's mark making will be projected onto the wall or screen.

Taking it forward

Have a go at:

- Letting the children create their mark making on the acetate sheet before they place the sheet onto the OHP.

What's in it for the children?

There is something very engaging for children to be able to see the marks that they are making magnified and projected onto a big space. The acetate is really easy to draw on, so can engage even reluctant mark makers.

Shadow drawing

What you need:

- **A light source** (lamp or the sun)
- **A selection of objects that cast interesting shadows**
- **Large pieces of paper**
- **Mark making tools such as pencils or felt tips**

What to do:

1. Place your objects in front of the light source.
2. Place a sheet of paper behind the objects.
3. Ask the children to draw around the shadow created by the light source, using the mark making tools provided.

Taking it forward

Have a go at:

- Making the shadow much bigger, for increased gross motor development.
- Using much smaller or thinner items for increased fine motor development.
- Using transparent items such as coloured water in bottles, or Perspex bricks, which will throw out colour when they cast a shadow.

What's in it for the children?

The children will learn how a shadow is created. In addition, being given a guide or outline to follow when mark making will require concentration, dexterity and control.

PVA in a builder's tray

What you need:

- PVA glue
- Large builder's tray or 'tuff spot'
- Warm soapy water

What to do:

1. Pour the glue into the middle of the tray and watch it spread.
2. Encourage the children to spread the glue with the palms of their hands.
3. Ask the children to create patterns, pictures and symbols in the glue using their index fingers.
4. Make sure they wash their hands when finished!

Taking it forward

Have a go at:

- Setting the height of the builder's tray or tuff spot to just above children's waist height. This will encourage the children to stretch their upper body rather than bend at the waist.
- Add some colour to your glue. You can use ready-mixed paint, food colouring or watered-down watercolour paint.

What's in it for the children?

In this idea, the children will be given plenty of opportunities to mark make using both gross and fine motor skills. As the glue is lovely and sticky you can encourage the children to press their palms and fingers together and pull them apart. Although this isn't strictly speaking mark making, it will help them to develop their mark making muscles.

Marshmallow paint

What you need:

- A microwave
- One cup of marshmallows
- Microwave-safe bowl
- Quarter of a cup of water
- Three tablespoons of golden syrup
- Paint pots or containers
- Food colouring or liquid watercolour paint

What to do:

1. Put one cup of marshmallows into a microwave-safe bowl.
2. Microwave on full power for 30 seconds.
3. Add the water and stir.
4. Microwave again for 30 seconds.
5. Add the golden syrup and stir.
6. Microwave a third and final time for 30 seconds.
7. Let the mixture cool and then separate out into your paint pots.
8. Add the food colouring and stir well.
9. Let the children get mark making! Remind them that the mixture is not for eating.

Taking it forward

Have a go at:

- Adding other textures to the paint, such as glitter.
- Asking the children to try painting with hands and fingers as well as brushes.

What's in it for the children?

The children can observe lots of science in action if you make this paint with them, especially when you microwave the marshmallows and they swell up! The paint also has a unique texture, which brings an added dimension to the mark making.

Woolly brushes

What you need:

- Odds and ends of balls of wool
- Sticks or bamboo canes
- Scissors

What to do:

1. Wrap the wool around one of your hands several times (but not so tight that you can't get it off in one movement).
2. Slip the wool off your hand, tie the ends and fold it in half (loops to the top) to create a 'V' shape.
3. Place a stick vertically at the bottom of the 'V'.
4. Use a length of wool to attach the stick to the bottom of the 'V', creating a woolly paintbrush.
5. Repeat with different amounts of wool on different-sized sticks.
6. Let the children paint with the woolly brushes!

Taking it forward

Have a go at:

- Using string or embroidery thread instead of wool.
- Changing the lengths of the loops to achieve different effects.
- Encouraging the children to try rolling the paint-loaded brush between their palms to create a 'splatter' effect.

What's in it for the children?

The bristles on the end of a conventional paintbrush make them relatively easy to control. The loops on the woolly brush make control more difficult and also give a very different outcome. The effect will change as the loops become more loaded with paint.

Ice chalk

What you need:

- One cup of cornflour
- One cup of water
- Food colouring or watered-down watercolour paint
- Ice lolly moulds

What to do:

1. Mix the cornflour and the water together well, stirring out any lumps.
2. If you want different colours of ice chalk, separate the mixture into different containers.
3. Add your chosen food colouring and mix well.
4. Pour into the lolly moulds and freeze for at least six hours.
5. Use the ice chalk to mark make with!

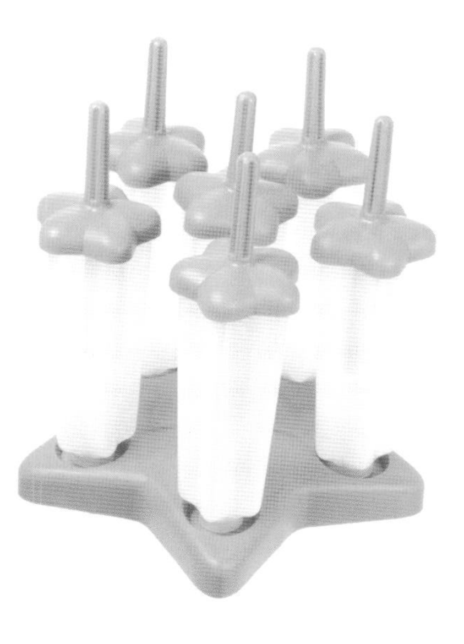

Taking it forward

- You can use this recipe to create lots of different shapes and sizes of chalk – you just need to change the shape and size of your mould.

What's in it for the children?

These chalks are great for mark making indoors and out, on both a small and a large scale. The children will be more inclined to mark make when they know that that are going to discover something exciting inside their chalk!

Discovery chalk

What you need:

- Quarter of a cup of warm water
- Half a cup of plaster of Paris
- Liquid watercolour paints or ready-mixed paint
- Muffin tin
- Small treasures such as gem stones or dinosaurs
- Access to a freezer

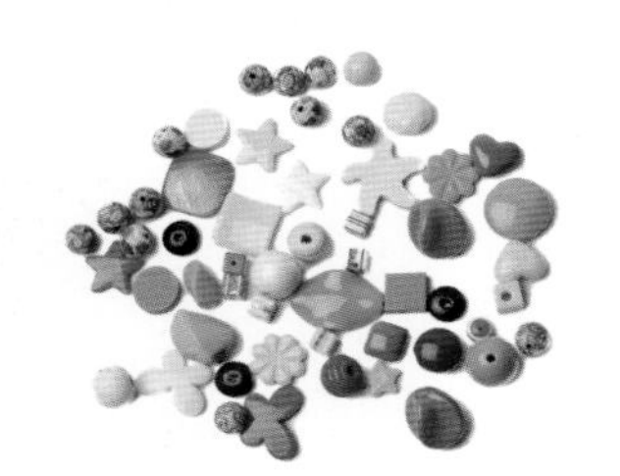

What to do:

1. Mix the warm water with the plaster of Paris.
2. Add a colour of your choice.
3. Pour a small amount into the bottom of your muffin tin.
4. Add the treasure.
5. Pour more plaster of Paris on top.
6. Leave to set overnight in a freezer.
7. Bring out of the freezer the next morning and encourage the children to mark make until the treasure in the chalk is uncovered!

Taking it forward

Have a go at:

- Using ice cube trays, if you haven't got ice lolly moulds.
- Making rainbow ice chalks by putting a small amount of coloured mixture into the bottom of a lolly mould. Let it partially freeze (an hour or so) then add a different colour on top. Repeat.

What's in it for the children?

The children will be able to observe the changing state of the ice melting into liquid form. The ice chalk also has a unique texture and will have a very different effect depending on the type of surface you are mark making on.

Summer snow

What you need:

- Shaving cream
- Baking tray
- Freezer
- Spatula or spoon

What to do:

1. Squirt shaving foam all over your baking tray.
2. Spread the foam out with your fingers.
3. Put the tray in the freezer and leave overnight.
4. Once you have taken it out of the freezer, use a spatula or spoon to break up the frozen foam.

Taking it forward

Have a go at:

- Mark making in your summer snow.
- Mark making on your summer snow, with paint, brushes and pipettes.
- Once the snow has melted, use the foam for mark making in and with.

What's in it for the children?

This is a great activity for encouraging children to mark make by experiencing texture. As the 'snow' melts, the texture continually changes, which in turn gives the children a whole new experience.

Top tip 

For best results, take the foam out of the freezer just before you need to use it.

Scratch and sniff paint

What you need:

- One cup of cornflour
- One cup of water
- Food colouring or watered-down watercolour paint
- Scents or essential oils
- A number of small containers

What to do:

1. Mix the cornflour and the water together well.
2. Separate your mixture into smaller containers, depending on how many colours you want.
3. Add a few drops of colour to each pot and stir well.
4. Add scents or essential oils to each pot and stir well.
5. Paint onto paper, and allow to dry.
6. Once dry, scratch and sniff your smelly picture!

Taking it forward

Have a go at:

- Making large-scale scratch and sniff pictures.
- Putting together a collage of the children's work to create a scratch and sniff garden.
- Using smells that aren't always nice (within reason!).

What's in it for the children?

This is a two-stage process. In the first stage, the children will be mixing their own paint and creating images, patterns and shapes. In the second stage they will be using their fine motor skills to scratch and trace the lines of their image.

Flower head splodge

What you need:

- Flower heads of different sizes
- Ready-mixed paint
- Small bowls or containers
- Paper

What to do:

1. Cut the flower heads, leaving enough stem for the children to hold the flowers.
2. Put different coloured paints into bowls or containers.
3. Dip the flower heads into the paint.
4. Either print or paint with the flower heads.

Taking it forward

Have a go at:

- Adding some petals to the paint while it is still wet.
- Mark making with other natural resources like moss or leaves.

What's in it for the children?

There is a lot to look at and talk about with the children before you even get to the mark making part of this activity. The children will need to think about how much paint they load onto the flower heads and how much pressure they need to use to make their prints without snapping or breaking the flower. All of these skills are essential for the children's mark making development.

Popping candy paint

What you need:

- A selection of ready-mixed paint
- Popping candy
- Fingers, brushes and paper
- Small bowls or containers

What to do:

1. Start by putting the popping candy and the paint in separate containers.
2. Dip your finger into the paint and then the popping candy.
3. Apply the 'popping paint' to paper.
4. See how long it takes for the paint to stop popping!

Taking it forward

Have a go at:

- Mixing some popping candy in with the paint before the children start painting. Can they finish before the candy stops popping?

What's in it for the children?

The fact that the paint 'pops' provides an extra level of engagement and intrigue. Younger children will be able to explore the texture and the noise of the popping paint as they mark make with it. Older children will enjoy the challenge of 'paint until the pop stops!'

Frozen foam paint

What you need:

- Shaving foam
- Food colouring or paint
- Small containers
- Scents or essential oils (optional)
- Small containers
- A freezer

What to do:

1. Mix some shaving foam, colour and any scent in a small pot.
2. Repeat until you have a selection of colours.
3. Place your pots in the freezer overnight.
4. Take out of the freezer immediately before use.
5. As the paint melts, observe how the texture changes.
6. Use the paint to mark make on a variety of different surfaces.

Taking it forward

Have a go at:

- Adding other ingredients to your paint, such as glitter or sequins.
- Melting with hands and applying with fingers.

What's in it for the children?

This paint offers children the opportunity to explore a number of textures, as well as observing the changing state of the paint as it moves from a solid to a liquid. If you want children to mark make on a far more gross motor scale, make these paints using larger containers.

Health & Safety

Never leave children unsupervised with essential oils.

Epsom salt sand

What you need:

- **Epsom salts** (can be substituted with table salt)
- **Freezer bags**
- **Food colouring or liquid watercolour paint**
- **Scents or essential oils** (optional)

What to do:

Depending on how much 'salt sand' you want:

1. Put the Epsom salts into a sealable freezer bag.
2. Add two or three drops of your chosen scent.
3. Add three or four drops of food colouring or liquid watercolour to the bag.
4. Seal the bag and then agitate the salt inside until it is completely covered.
5. If you want a stronger colour, add more drops of food colouring.
6. Repeat the process until you have all of the colours that you want.
7. Put your coloured salt sand onto sheets of black paper and get mark making!

Taking it forward

Have a go at:

- Putting your salt onto a light box to make shapes and patterns.
- Asking the children to paint pictures with glue and then sprinkle the salt over the top.

What's in it for the children?

Epsom salts have a particularly nice texture to work with and are different from table salt. I have found that the children really enjoy the process of creating the salt sand, especially agitating the bag and watching the salt change colour. Just make sure that you have sealed the bags well!

Health & Safety

Never leave children unsupervised with essential oils.

Magnetic slime

What you need:

- Two cups of cornflour
- Hot water
- Two cups of PVA glue
- Two tablespoons of iron oxide powder
- Measuring cups
- Two mixing bowls
- Magnets

What to do:

1. Place two cups of cornflour into the first mixing bowl.
2. Add one and a half cups of hot water and stir.
3. In the second mixing bowl, put two cups of PVA glue.
4. Add two tablespoons of iron oxide powder to the PVA.
5. Add one and a half cups of water to the PVA and iron oxide mixture.
6. Add the contents of the first bowl to the second bowl.
7. Stir, stir and keep stirring until it comes together like slime (this can take a couple of minutes)!
8. Use the magnets to mark make in your magnetic slime.

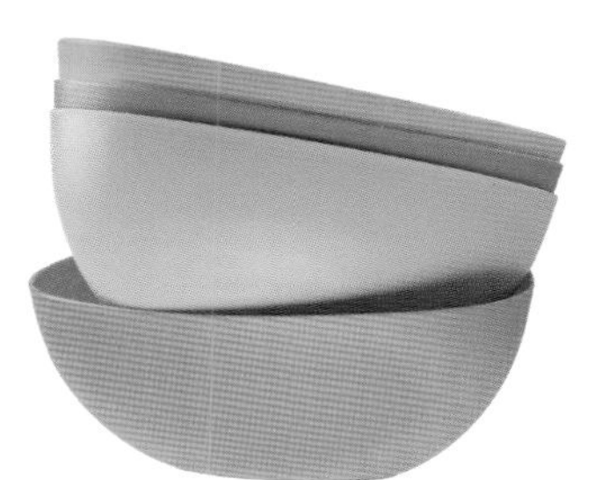

Taking it forward

Have a go at:

- Using the magnets to attract the slime to make patterns and shapes.
- Experimenting with different-sized magnets.

What's in it for the children?

This is a real 'sciencey' experiment, but one that never fails to engage the children. Although some of the ingredients might not be familiar to you, they are all readily available and easy to use – so have a go!

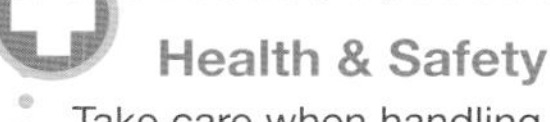

Health & Safety

Take care when handling hot liquids.

Magnetic sand

What you need:

- **Plain or coloured sand** (make your own coloured sand – see page 56)
- **Iron oxide powder**
- **A shallow tray on legs**
- **Magnets**

What to do:

1. Mix one cup of sand with one tablespoon of iron oxide powder.
2. Place your sand on a shallow tray.
3. Use magnets on the underside of the tray to make patterns, shapes and symbols with the sand.

Taking it forward

Have a go at:

- Using a smaller tray and supporting it on an upside-down box with one side cut out so children can use their magnets on the underside of the tray.
- Mixing other small magnetic items into the sand.

What's in it for the children?

As well as exploring magnetism, the children will be 'virtual' mark making. Although they will be using all of the muscles they need to make a mark, the symbols, patterns and shapes will be represented by the moving sand rather than being made *in* the sand.

Fluorescent rice

What you need:

- White rice
- Freezer bags
- Baking parchment
- Fluorescent paint
- Black light or bulb

What to do:

1. Put one cup of rice in a freezer bag.
2. Add a squirt of fluorescent paint (it's always better to start with less).
3. Seal the bag and agitate until all of the rice is covered.
4. Pour onto a sheet of baking parchment and spread out to dry.
5. Repeat until you have all of the colours you need.
6. In a dark space, spread out the rice, switch on your black light and watch it glow!
7. The children can create shapes, patterns and symbols in the glowing rice.

Taking it forward

Have a go at:

- Using the fluorescent paint and fingers or paintbrushes for 'glow in the dark' mark making.
- Encourage the children to use a paintbrush to move the rice around – this will help them to develop their fine motor dexterity and grip.

What's in it for the children?

The fact that this rice glows in the dark always brings with it a high level of engagement. The texture of the rice as the children move it with their hands and fingers adds another dimension to this activity.

Edible marshmallow sticks

What you need:

- Marshmallows
- Drinking straws
- Honey
- Hundreds and thousands
- Small paintbrushes
- A small pot
- A plate
- Baking parchment

What to do:

1. Stick a drinking straw into the top of each marshmallow.
2. Put the hundreds and thousands onto a plate.
3. Put the honey into a small pot.
4. Using a small paintbrush, paint the bottom of the marshmallow.
5. Paint half way up the side, then stop.
6. Dip the marshmallow into the hundreds and thousands to coat the bottom.
7. Turn the marshmallow onto its side and roll to coat.
8. Put onto the baking parchment – or just eat it!

Taking it forward

Have a go at:

- Using smaller brushes for an even bigger challenge.
- Using cocktail sticks instead of straws, and mini marshmallows.

What's in it for the children?

Food is a great motivator! Even though this activity can be tricky, the children will stick with it for the end result. It is important that they show some control while they are painting on the honey and don't just 'dunk', as the painting is where the skill development is going to come from.

Styrofoam mono prints

What you need:

- A takeaway container or styrofoam tile
- Blunt pencils or play dough tools
- Ready-mixed paint
- Tray
- Small paint roller
- Paper

What to do:

1. Cut your takeaway container in half and then trim off the sides.
2. Using the blunt pencil or tool, draw by pressing into the styrofoam.
3. Coat your roller with paint.
4. Roll over the top of your design.
5. Place paper on top of your styrofoam print.
6. Rub the paper gently with your hand.
7. Peel back to reveal your work of art!

Taking it forward

Have a go at:

- Creating styrofoam mark making on a much larger scale.
- Joining the prints together to create a collage.

What's in it for the children?

There are several processes involved in this mark making activity and no two attempts are exactly the same. The children will have to use different amounts of pressure to be able to create their patterns and marks, which is great for fine motor development.

Chopping board mark making

What you need:

- **A glass chopping board or mirror** (you can also use a baking tray, turned upside-down)
- **Ready-mixed paint**
- **Paper**

What to do:

1. Squirt some paint onto the chopping board.
2. Spread the paint out with your fingers (or a paintbrush).
3. Use hands and fingers to mark make in the paint.
4. Lay a sheet of paper onto your chopping board.
5. Gently rub the back of the paper.
6. Peel off to reveal a print of the artwork!

Taking it forward

Have a go at:

- Going large-scale and using a table top instead of a chopping board.
- Using a chopping board straight from the fridge or freezer.
- Using a chopping board that has been sitting in hot water.
- Using cotton buds instead of fingers for the mark making.

What's in it for the children?

For emergent mark makers, this activity allows them to practise making shapes and patterns easily as there is little resistance from the glass and the paint. For more advanced mark makers, the use of a cotton bud requires a far higher level of dexterity and skill and therefore is a greater challenge.

Fizzy pictures

What you need:

- One cup of table salt
- One cup of bicarbonate of soda
- PVA glue
- Food colouring
- Food colouring
- Vinegar
- Paper
- Pipette
- Paintbrush or squeezy dispenser

What to do:

1. Mix the salt and the bicarbonate of soda together.
2. Paint a picture with a brush or fingers using just the PVA, or alternatively put the PVA into a squeezy dispenser and 'dribble' a picture!
3. Pour the salt and bicarbonate mix over the glue picture.
4. Shake off the excess and leave to dry.
5. When dry, drip food colouring onto the salt and bicarbonate mix on your picture, and watch the colours spread.
6. Drip vinegar onto your picture and watch the colours fizz!

Taking it forward

Have a go at:

- Adding food colouring to the glue before you paint with it.
- Creating some 'blobs' of glue that will give you a big fizz.
- Mixing some bicarbonate of soda into your glue as well as dusting it on the top.

What's in it for the children?

Painting with glue offers a lower level dexterity challenge if you are using a large brush. The smaller the brush, the more challenging the task will be.

Using a sauce dispenser full of glue requires the children to squeeze to produce their picture. This action will also impact on their fine motor dexterity.

Ice lolly fizzer

What you need:

- Ready-mixed paint
- Bicarbonate of soda
- Ice lolly tray
- Vinegar
- Small bowls

Taking it forward

Have a go at:

- Replacing the vinegar when the lollies stop fizzing.
- Mixing bicarbonate of soda and paint together, mark make and allow the paintings to dry. Then drip vinegar onto the paintings and watch them fizz.

What to do:

1. Mix your paint with a little water to make it the consistency of single cream.
2. Fill each of your ice lolly moulds half-full of bicarbonate of soda.
3. Slowly add the paint and water mixture, and stir well.
4. Freeze overnight.
5. Pour vinegar into a small bowl/s.
6. Dip your 'ice lolly' into the vinegar so that it fizzes, then paint with it!

What's in it for the children?

Again, with this activity the children are able to observe some science taking place in front of them as well as being motivated to make marks before the fizz runs out.

Chalkboard canvas or tea tray

What you need:

- Shop-bought canvases or wooden trays
- Blackboard paint
- Radiator roller

What to do:

1. Paint your canvases or tea tray with several coats of blackboard paint.
2. Use a roller for the best finish.
3. Once dry, the boards are ready to use. Mark make with chalk.
4. Once done, wash with a damp cloth and reuse.

Taking it forward

Have a go at:

- Making some huge canvases for collaborative artwork.
- Using the blackboard paint as a background for working with found materials such as pebbles, leaves and feathers.

What's in it for the children?

The canvases make instant art that the children can hang and re-hang each time. The tea tray is portable and can be moved around the setting.

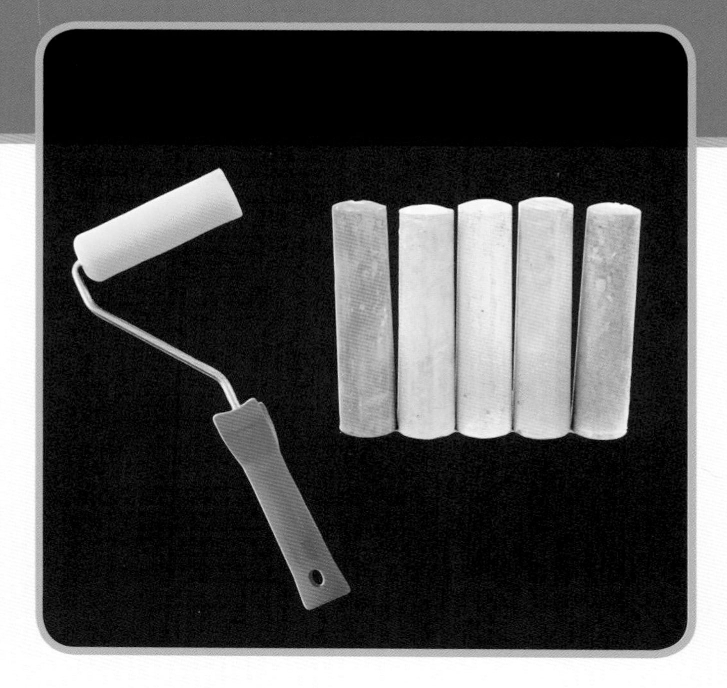

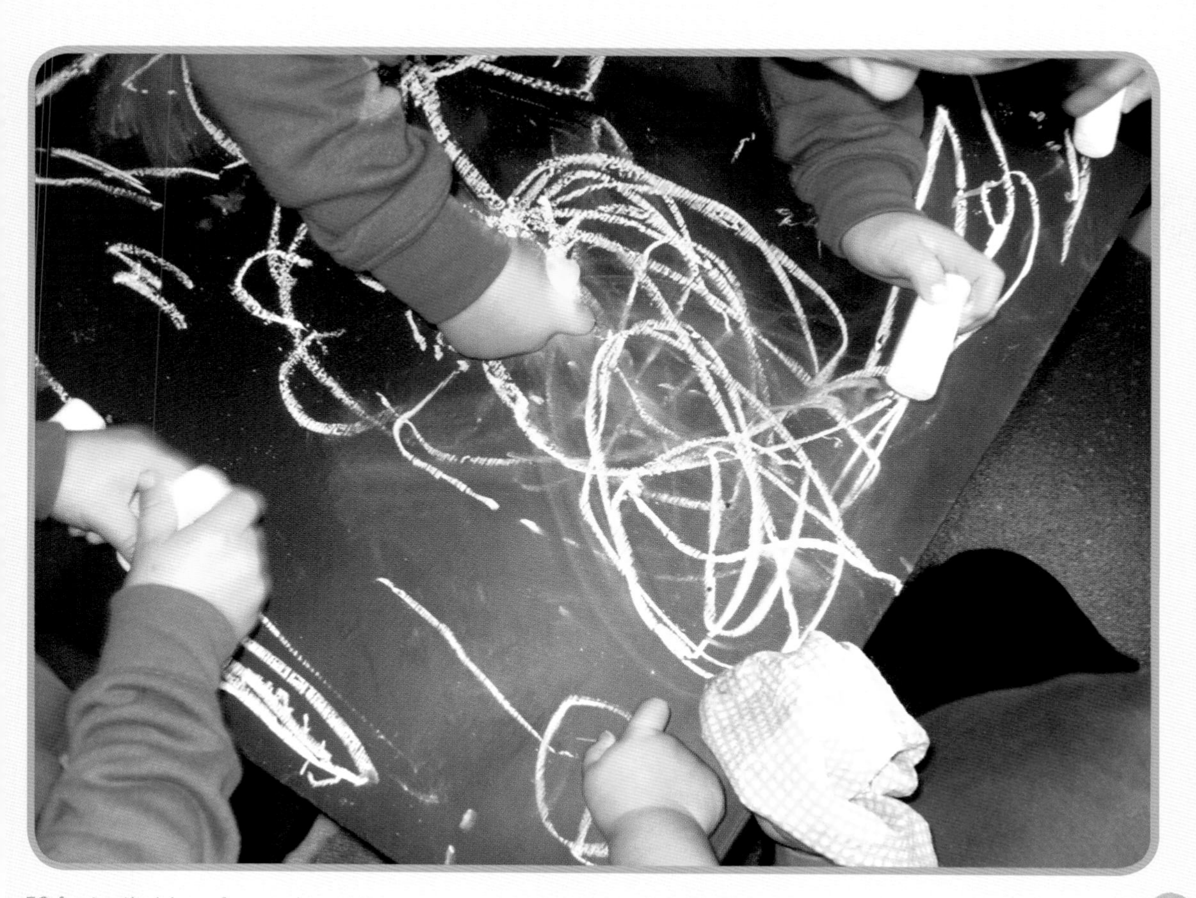

Clean dirt!

What you need:

- Bicarbonate of soda
- Black or brown food colouring
- Drop of water

What to do:

1. Use as much bicarbonate of soda as you want.
2. Pour the bicarbonate into a large bowl.
3. Add the food colouring, a few drops at a time.
4. Stir with a metal spoon (to avoid staining wooden spoons).
5. Keep adding and stirring until your 'dirt' is the desired colour.
6. To enhance the multi-sensory experience, the children may wish to add other substances such as glitter or flower petals.
7. Add a few drops of water (if needed) to create a realistic soil texture.
8. Encourage the children to mark make in the 'dirt'.

Taking it forward

Have a go at:

- Adding other enhancements to your dirt, such as small pebbles, leaves and roots.
- Making large quantities of clean dirt and use it as an enhancement to your sand and water play.
- Adding vinegar to your dirt and watch it fizz!

What's in it for the children?

This is a great activity for exploring texture, as well as encouraging both gross and fine motor mark making. If the children add water to their dirt they can observe how the substance changes.

Peg fan

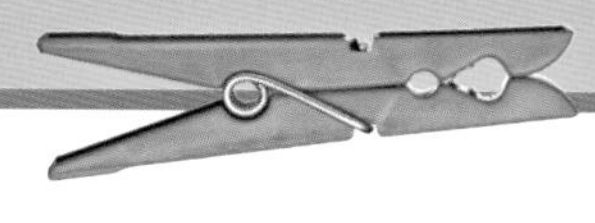

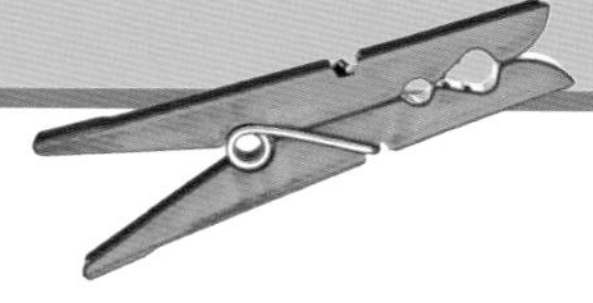

What you need:

- Seven clothes pegs
- A glue gun
- Felt tip pens
- Paper

What to do:

1. Glue the pegs together, long side against long side.
2. When the glue is set, clip a felt tip into each of the pegs.
3. Holding your peg fan in the middle, draw with all of the pegs at once.

Taking it forward

Have a go at:

- Trying different numbers of pegs – anything from two pegs upwards works.
- Holding the peg fan in both hands when you are mark making.

What's in it for the children?

Because the children are not directly holding the felt tips and they are making multiple marks at once, this activity requires a higher level of dexterity. Children can find it challenging to keep all of the felt tips level and moving at the same time.

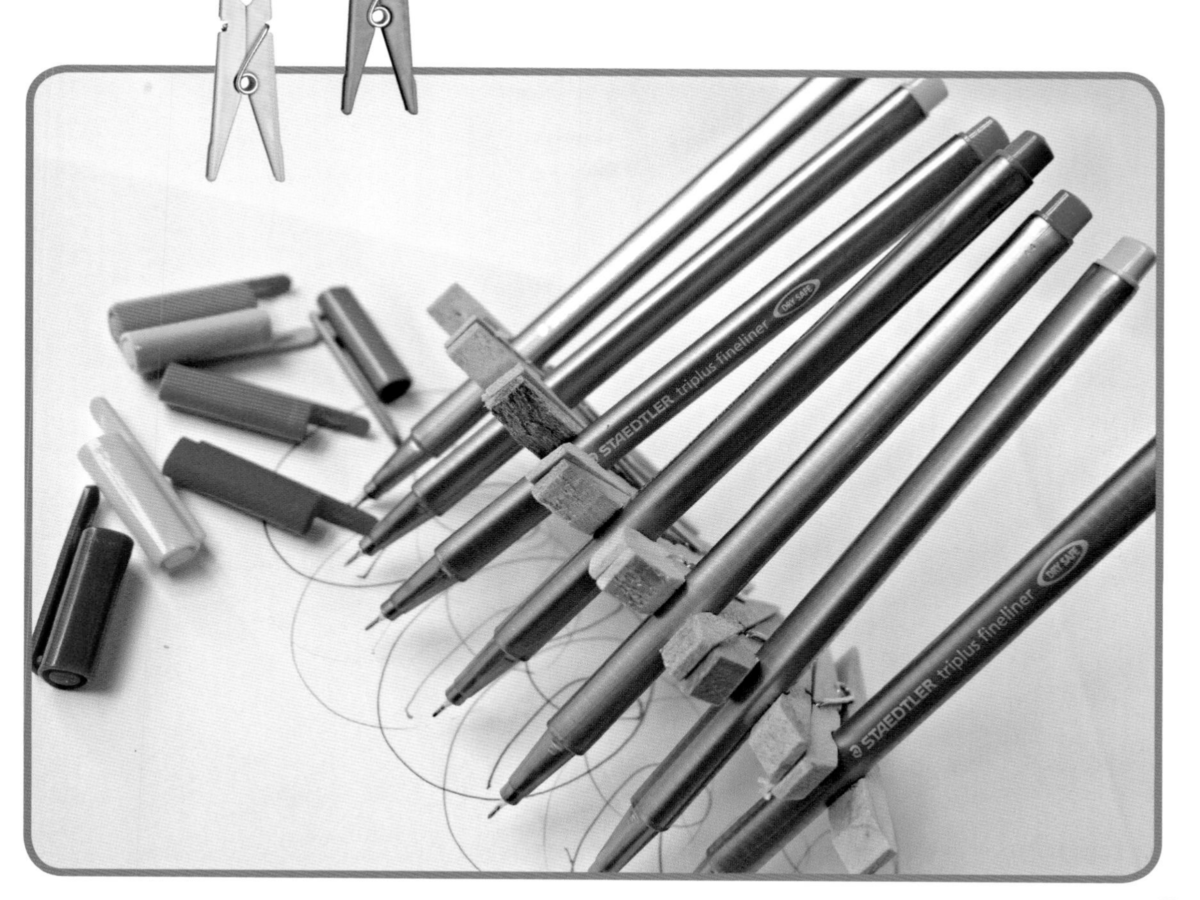

Bingo dabber

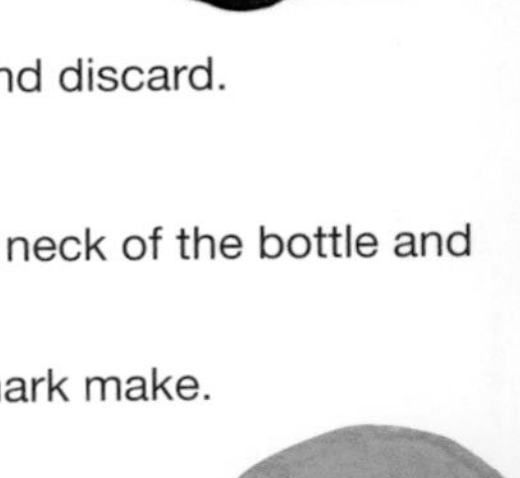

What you need:

- Small clear travel bottles
- Make-up sponges
- Elastic bands
- Paint

What to do:

1. Take the lid off the travel bottles and discard.
2. Fill each bottle with paint.
3. Place a make-up sponge over the neck of the bottle and secure with an elastic band.
4. Turn the bottles upside down to mark make.

Taking it forward

Have a go at:

- Making giant bingo dabbers by using larger bottles.
- Filling your bottles with paint of different consistencies for different effects.

What's in it for the children?

The children can make these bingo dabbers themselves once they have been shown what to do. Depending on the size of the bottle, the children will be either consolidating their palm grip or developing their tripod grip – not to mention having fun!

Window squeegee

What you need:

- **A large flat surface** (such as a table top)
- **Ready mixed paint**
- **Window squeegees**
- **Large sheets of paper** (optional, for relief print)

What to do:

1. Squirt paint liberally onto your flat surface.
2. Let the children use the squeegees to move the paint around.
3. Experiment with the different marks you can make with the squeegee.
4. Add more colours of paint as you go along.
5. Take a relief print of the finished work (optional).

Taking it forward

Have a go at:

- Using smaller utensils and fingers to mark make in the paint once the children have finished their squeegee pictures.

What's in it for the children?

This is a great opportunity for children to experiment with large-scale colour mixing as well as developing their upper body skills, gross motor movement and dexterity.

Cocktail stick draggers

What you need:

- Thick cardboard
- Cocktail sticks
- Glue or sticky tape
- Paint
- A shallow tray or saucer
- Paper, dough or clay

What to do:

1. Cut a rectangle of card (small for a few sticks, large for lots of sticks).
2. Using glue or sticky tape, attach cocktail sticks to the card so that two thirds of each stick is visible – make sure all of the sticks are the same length.
3. Stick another rectangle of card on top of the first one for strength (you will have created a cocktail stick sandwich!).
4. Pour some paint into your shallow container.
5. Dip your cocktail sticks into the paint.
6. Drag the cocktail sticks across the paper to make marks, patterns and symbols.

Taking it forward

Have a go at:

- Dragging the sticks through dough or clay to make marks.
- Making a larger version using skewers.
- Making an outdoor version using twigs.

What's in it for the children?

This is a unique mark making activity for the children; as there is no 'handle' on their dragger, they will have to grip it horizontally and use their wrist to help them to manipulate it. The children will also have to control of the amount of pressure that they are using. If they use too little then there will be no mark; if they use too much then the sticks will snap.

Health & Safety

Children will need to be supervised when using the cocktail sticks as they can be quite sharp.

Felt tip cars

What you need:

- Toy cars
- Felt tip pens or chalk
- Masking tape
- A large flat surface
- A large piece of paper

What to do:

1. Using masking tape, attach a felt tip pen to the back of a toy car (make sure that the tip of the pen is adjacent to the wheels of the car and will touch the paper when the lid is off and the car is set down on the paper).
2. Run the cars all over the paper to make marks, lines and symbols.

Taking it forward

Have a go at:

- Adding a felt tip pen to the front and back of the car.
- Joining cars together to make multiple marks.

What's in it for the children?

There is usually a lot of engagement with this activity because it involves cars! The children will be using their fingers rather than their palms to help them to navigate the cars, which will have a positive impact on their mark making ability.

Paper towel art

What you need:

- Newspaper
- Food colouring or liquid watercolour paints
- Small containers
- White paper towels
- Pipettes

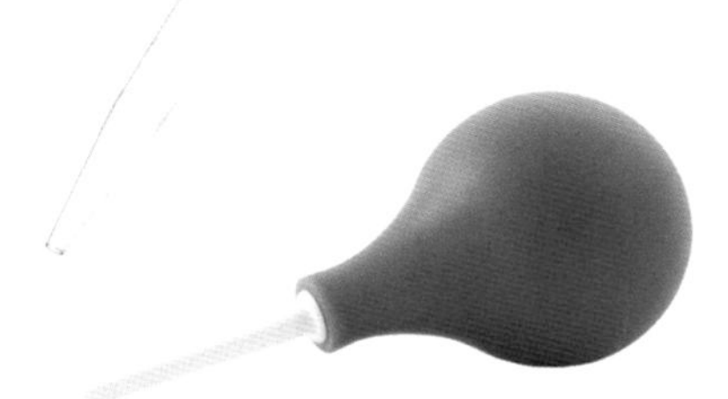

What to do:

1. Put a few sheets of newspaper down on the surface that you will be working on.
2. Separate your food colouring or liquid watercolour into small containers.
3. Lay a sheet of paper towel on top of your newspaper.
4. Use the pipettes to suck up a small amount of colour.
5. Drop the colour in different spots on your paper towel.
6. Continue until the paper is covered.

Taking it forward

Have a go at:

- Folding the paper towel in half before you start, for some symmetrical mark making.
- Dampening the paper towel before you start for a different effect.
- Using the patterned towels in other aspects of children's creativity.

What's in it for the children?

The children will be making indiscriminate marks with this activity. The skill is all in the controlled use of the pipette. The children will be able to see that the marks they make will change depending on how much pressure they apply.

Paint, pompoms and pegs

What you need:

- **Small pots**
- **Ready-mixed paint**
- **Pompoms** (various sizes)
- **Pegs**
- **Paper**

Taking it forward

Have a go at:

- Using different-sized pompoms for different effects.
- Using fingers instead of pegs to hold the pompoms without getting any paint on them!

What's in it for the children?

This activity is good for pattern and colour mixing, as well as getting children working on their pincer grip and muscle control to allow them to effectively pick up the pompoms and then print with them.

What to do:

1. Decant a small amount of paint into a number of small containers.
2. Spread the pompoms out next to your working area.
3. Using a peg, pick up a pompom.
4. Dip the pompom into some paint.
5. Print with the pompom onto the paper.
6. Repeat until you have finished.

Tin twang

What you need:

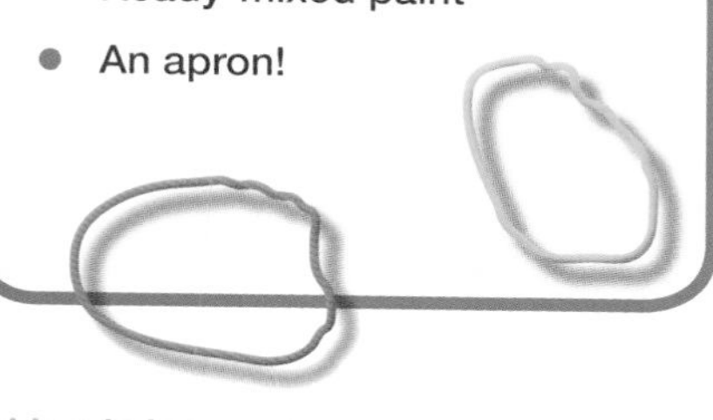

- Newspaper
- Paper
- Baking tray
- Elastic bands
- Ready-mixed paint
- An apron!

What to do:

1. Put down sheets of newspaper around the work space.
2. Cut out a piece of paper to fit the bottom of your tray.
3. Place the paper in the bottom of the tray.
4. Stretch elastic bands around the tray, in any direction.
5. Put a small amount of paint onto the section of each elastic band that is suspended over the paper.
6. Use your fingers to 'twang' the elastic band and splatter the paint over the paper.
7. Carefully remove the elastic bands and leave your splatter pictures to dry.

Taking it forward

Have a go at:

- Using different-sized trays and different-sized elastic bands, for varied effects.
- Taking the activity outdoors on a large scale, using a builder's tray and lengths of elastic.

What's in it for the children?

The children are having the opportunity to experiment with colour and colour mixing. They are also experiencing cause and effect as they 'twang' the elastic bland. The manipulation of the band will also really support their fine motor development.

Double brush painting

What you need:

- Chopstick helpers or training chopsticks
- Paintbrushes
- Small pots
- Ready-mixed paint, food colouring or liquid watercolour paint
- Paper

What to do:

1. Insert two paintbrushes into your chopstick helpers.
2. Dip each brush into a separate colour of paint, or squeeze them together and dip them both into one.
3. Once the brushes are loaded with colour, begin painting on the paper.

Taking it forward

Have a go at:

- Using different-sized brushes in each side of the chopstick helpers.
- Practising squeezing the brushes in and out as you paint with them.
- Putting a pair of brushes in both hands and paint with two hands at once.

What's in it for the children?

Because they are painting with two brushes at once in just one hand, you are really challenging children's fine motor dexterity here. Squeezing the brushes as they paint will also help to develop pincer grip and control. If children have brushes in both hands they will be challenging their dexterity and bilateral brain function!

Smelly sand paint

What you need:

- **Play sand**
- **Ready-mixed paint** (several colours)
- **Pots**
- **Essential oils or scent**
- **Tin foil**

What to do:

1. Mix a good amount of play sand into the pots of paint.
2. Add some drops of essence or scent.
3. Stir well.
4. Lay some tin foil onto a flat surface.
5. Mark make!

Taking it forward

Have a go at:

- Introducing other utensils to make patterns in your smelly sand paint.
- Painting with smelly sand paint on different surfaces such as paper, cardboard or sandpaper.

What's in it for the children?

There is a lovely sensory element to this activity both in colour, texture and scent. The tin foil not only adds a reflective dimension to the mark making, it also allows the paint to move really easy. For more of a challenge, spread the paint on different surfaces.

Health & Safety

Never leave children unsupervised with essential oils.

Ice painting

What you need:

- Shallow bowl or tray
- Water
- Freezer
- Paint or food colouring
- Paint brushes or pipettes

What to do:

1. Fill the bowl or tray with about 2cm of water.
2. Freeze for at least 8 hours – overnight works well.
3. Take your bowl or tray out of the freezer.
4. Turn the ice out of the bowl or tray.
5. Place the ice onto a flat surface (indoors or out).
6. Paint onto the ice using brushes, or drop on food colouring using pipettes.
7. Watch how your marks change as the ice melts.

Taking it forward

Have a go at:

- Using a much larger tray or bowl if you have the freezer space.
- Adding salt or warm water to the paint and the food colouring, then watching the effect of the new marks on the ice.
- Sprinkling salt on the existing marks.

What's in it for the children?

The children will have the opportunity to experience how water can change state when it is frozen. Mark making on ice has a very different texture compared to mark making on paper. The children can also manipulate how the marks change by adding salt or warm water.

Musical mark making

What you need:

- **Paintbrushes, pencils or felt tips**
- **Pipe cleaners**
- **Paint** (if using paintbrushes)
- **Jingle bells**

What to do:

1. Thread the bells onto a pipe cleaner. Use several bells on some pipe cleaners, and single bells on others.
2. Wrap the pipe cleaners around the end of the paintbrushes, pencils or felt tips and secure by twisting.
3. Mark make!

Taking it forward

Have a go at:

- Using long and short strokes with the musical mark makers to create different sounds.
- Dabbing the paint brushes for a different techniques and a different sounds.
- Mark making on both horizontal and vertical surfaces.

What's in it for the children?

The children will need to use different levels of dexterity depending on the length and thickness of the mark making implements you provide. They will have to manipulate their tools in a variety of ways to make the bells jingle. This will help them to develop their fine motor dexterity.

Puffy sand paint

What you need:

- Shaving cream
- Bowls
- Play sand
- Food colouring or liquid watercolour
- Spoons
- Paintbrushes
- Paper

What to do:

1. Squirt shaving foam into each of the bowls.
2. Add two or three large spoonfuls of sand.
3. Add a couple of drops of food colouring.
4. Stir well.
5. Using spoons or paintbrushes, 'dollop' your puffy sand paint onto your paper.
6. Spread with hands, fingers or paintbrushes.

Taking it forward

Have a go at:

- Adding different quantities of sand to achieve different textures.
- Adding other textures, such as soil or tea leaves.

What's in it for the children?

This is a great activity for exploring texture, as well as encouraging both gross and fine motor mark making. The making of the paint involves lots of spooning and stirring, and the application of the puffy paint will utilise and develop children's dexterity skills.

Gloop slime

What you need:

- A bowl or tray
- Cornflour
- Bubble bath
- Green food colouring
- Pipettes

What to do:

1. Cover the bottom of the bowl or tray with a layer of cornflour.
2. Add a few drops of green food colouring to the bubble bath to make it slime-coloured!
3. Using the pipettes, add the green bubble mixture to the cornflour.
4. Use your fingers and hands to combine the mixtures and mark make at the same time.

Taking it forward

Have a go at:

- Trying other colours of bubble bath.
- Using a larger tray for more emergent mark makers.
- Adding other resources to the slime once it is fully mixed and encouraging the children to pick the objects out.

What's in it for the children?

For children who are engaging in gross motor mark making, there is lots of scope for moving the slime around with their hands and working on their upper bodies and shoulder pivots. The more dexterous mark makers will need to use their fingers to manipulate the pipettes and then mix the slime.

Homemade powder paint

What you need:

- Playground chalks
- Ziplock freezer bags
- A builder's tray or large shallow container
- A hammer

What to do:

1. Put all of the chalks of one colour in a ziplock bag.
2. Hammer the bag until the chalk becomes powder.

Either:

3. Pour the powder into a builder's tray or shallow container and encourage the children to use their hands and fingers to mark make in it.

Or:

4. Add water to your powder to create your own paint.

Taking it forward

Have a go at:

- Letting the children experiment with creating their own paint from the chalk powder.
- Mixing the powders to create new colours before adding water.

What's in it for the children?

The action of hitting the chalk in the bag with the hammer is impacting on their hand eye coordination as well as their fine and gross motor dexterity. Manipulating the mark making resources or using their fingers and hands will further develop their grip.

Chocolate mousse mark making

What you need:

- Polythene sheeting, a large plastic folder or a large mirror
- Individual chocolate mousse or powdered packet desert
- Sticky tape

What to do:

1. Cut the polythene sheeting to A3 size (or alternatively use a plastic folder). Alternatively, using a mirror will help the children develop an understanding of control and mark making formation.
2. Tape the polythene sheet to the table.
3. Make up your powdered desert and allow it to set.
4. Give each child a large spoonful of desert and let them mark make on the plastic with it.

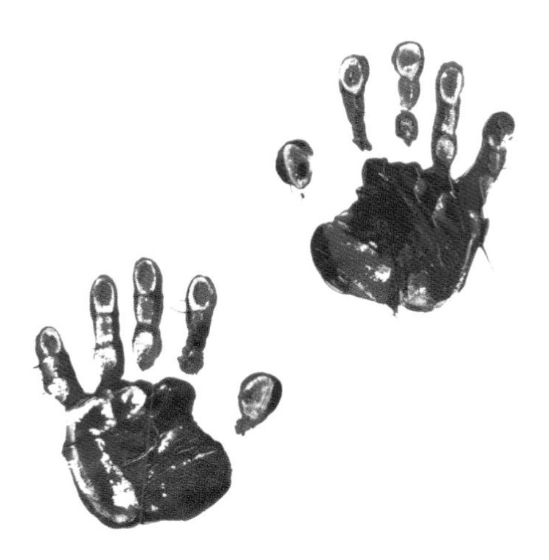

Taking it forward

Have a go at:

- Using different flavours of desert in different colours for a multi-sensory experience.
- Providing a selection of smaller mark making tools such as cotton buds or cocktail sticks.
- Inserting patterns or shapes under your polythene for the children to trace.

What's in it for the children?

Who wouldn't want to mark make in chocolate?! Make sure that the size of the polythene and the mark making resources match the dexterity of the children to ensure that the activity is impacting on the appropriate stage of development.

Deconstructed role play

What you need:

- Lots of cardboard boxes and open-ended resources
- Sheets of paper or a roll of lining paper
- Felt tip pens

What to do:

1. Create an open-ended role play area with cardboard boxes, tubes, crates and other open-ended resources.
2. Back the wall behind your role play area (at child height) with plain paper.
3. Allow the children to draw on the paper to create 'features' and a backdrop for their own role play.

Taking it forward

Have a go at:

- Introducing elements from this idea into other areas for provision, such as small world play.
- Encouraging the children to draw and label the illustrations that they are using in their play.

What's in it for the children?

Apart from the engagement that children will get from being able to structure their own play, they often respond very well to the freedom and control of being able to create their own individual backdrops.